# IF I WERE OTHER THAN MYSELF

For Mark, Danny, Tasha, Holly and Mum,
without whom none of these pages
would have been written.

Published by TROIKA

First published 2020

Troika Books Ltd
Well House, Green Lane, Ardleigh CO7 7PD
www.troikabooks.com

Text and illustrations copyright
© Sue Hardy-Dawson 2020

The moral rights of the
author/illustrator have been asserted

All rights reserved

A CIP catalogue record for this book
is available from the British Library

ISBN 978-1-909991-85-9

1 3 5 7 9 10 8 6 4 2

Printed in Poland

# IF I WERE
## OTHER
## THAN MYSELF

**Poems and Illustrations
by Sue Hardy-Dawson**

troika

# CONTENTS

# Book Thief

I've stolen stories from a wishing well
taken tales from a lion that could speak
I've hitched with a witch
used straw to stitch
seen a mountain's flare and a dragon's teeth.

I've kept a kiss for a sleeping princess
made off with a crown from a unicorn
I've travelled the waves
on a mermaid's tail
felt the earth shake beneath a dinosaur.

I've opened doors into magic trees
picked the lock on a giant's oak chest
I've trespassed on roads
made of fine fairy gold
stowed away in a green ogre's nest.

I've taken a thorn from a tiger's toe
swiped a rare pirates' map for a dare
I've had sandwiches too
with a bear from Peru
yet they swear I've stayed in this chair...

## Seamstress

Each night I pull threads of birds
shake them loose; unpick the sky's

dappled husks of thrush and wren
mulberry silk from blackbird eyes

unlacing swathed, loops of swifts
tangled ropes of swallows' flight

I wind wet weather on to spools
collect the crystal beads of rain

unknot sleet, smooth soft snow
roll rainbows, onto coloured skeins.

Lastly, smoggy chimney smoke
chalky trails from tails of planes.

I clean and press, sew, repair
bring out sky's box; put away

strips of darkness; unpinned stars
fraying shadows, darned in grey

Then I card, spin; weave again
and sit up till dawn, stitching day.

# Legends of Bears

We have heard of those
great northern bears
big as glaciers
dark eyes hovering
a storm that bites.

There are rumours of snow
with mouths wide as caves
sharpened icicles
such terrible teeth
death floating on ice.

Or so we are told
their claws; made to tear
a blizzard that mauls
and those still swearing
that many do hide

under iceberg flows
in fissures that grow
forever winter
with soundless feet
though it may be lies.

Believe them? Who knows?
But often one stares
feels unearthly chills.
Penguin foreboding?
A trick of the white?

*Poles apart, this poem was inspired by a joke: do penguins believe in polar bears?*

# The Girl Who Ate Sunshine

Once a girl ate the night
spun it like sugar
unfolded the moon
till pale as rice paper
then sifted its tail
with a fork from the sea.
And with each spoonful
she slowly grew dimmer.

*Moonlight,* she said, *is no good for me.*

Once a girl ate the dawn
peppered with shadow
gently she pared
the darkness away
then licked its crumbs
up from the  meadow
and with every mouthful
felt greyer and grimmer.

*Half-light*, she said, *is hardly for me.*

But inside the sun rose
speckled with daisies.
Filled her and warmed
all tiny bright things.
Then as she walked
all days grew sweeter
and with every footstep
she felt the earth singing.

*Sunshine*, she said,
*is the food for me.*

# A Dark Tale

Once on a moonless, starless night
in the total absence of light
where the clouds hung heavy as bricks
in a mist so thick it could stick
under the

    drip

       drip

          drip

of a creaking, crumbling bridge, dank
below the grimy grassy banks
and jet shadows of blank water
of the black and greasy river
beneath the

    deep

       deep

          deep

rocking of the cold and murky drift
of faceless ghosts of sleeping fish
down further still than silent dreams
of slimy pebbles, gloomy weeds
it was so

very

very

very

dark...

# The Invisible Net Maker

How they smiled when he asked
for a piece of the wind
how they laughed very loud
when he raced after clouds
mocked, when he threaded at last
needles with air so thin
soon he'd drawn quite a crowd
and not one with a frown
as he caught them up fast
with a net none could see
but they're not laughing now
no there's hardly a sound.

# Casting Stones

Ah we are few now
but once our wolf song
was praised as earth and rain, long before
the tales of babes and wanderings in woods
of girls in scarlet hoods
lost and alone.

Almost silent now
yet our mountain song
dazzled stars and swelled moons, long before
rumours of sly dealings, the sheepish ruse
of a shepherd boy who
never came home.

Only echoes now
though our forest song
lulled leaf and greeted tree, long before
stories of sticks and straw, of howling air
of little pigs and their
houses blown down.

All but shades now
but for our wind song
yellowing bones. Oh don't get us wrong
we are big, we are bad, we have killed
but are you without guilt
you who cast stones?

## The Selkie Child

There's a girl on the cliff
with silver hair
softly she weeps
awake yet asleep
but if you ask her
what she does there
unhearing she'll stare
out into the deep
singing her sweet song
as green as the sea.

*I'm the selkie child of a selkie bride*
*and the sea is brother and sister to me...*

Where the moon is abroad
and sands burnt white
above waters wild,
hear the selkie's child
calling her mother
by pale starlight
longing to reach
beyond broken tides
sending her wind words
far into the night.

*I'm a selkie child and here must I bide*
*whispering spells to the sea and sky...*

Yet below on the beach
there something stirs
seal shadows creep
in dark shades of dream
but if you ask them
what they do there
unhearing they'll stare
up from shingle and weed
singing their sad songs
all  begging her see.

*Come poor selkie child, hear your mother's cries*
*for we are the brothers and sisters you seek...*

# Problem Child

Miss said,
*We have a problem.*

I said, *Where?*
*I can't see a problem.*

She said,
*Let me explain*

and explained
very, very slowly
exactly what she saw
as the problem.

I said,
*I don't see that*
*as much of a problem.*

She said, *I know*
*that's the problem.*

# The Loneliest Boy

He always sits still
safe by the window
a desk holding down
his bird, hollow bones.

Dull eyes flit about
as if he's not there
under sleep heavy lids
smooth as milk moons.

I've tried to reach in
tried to find his smile
on lips with no words
for too solid things.

For deep in the dark
lost pools of his mind
he'll not come out
and I cannot climb in.

# The Always Child

In between the lines, lives the Halfway child
thin as a cloud
that shifts in the wind.
She is half rain
on nights grown wild
her voice half full, of fallen leaves.

But where all lines meet, bides an Always child
as stout as stone
all timbered skin.
He is both moon
and a wave held still
all the sighs and the swell of rising seas.

And where lines are drawn, is a Sometimes child
rubbing letters
until they fade.
She has some bright
and yet still some shade
the charcoal figments of summer dreams.

Where lines cross over, is the Only child
his only words
flat to the page.
His books are square
and he only reads
what he's told is there, for him to see.

And where no lines live, is the Nowhere child
who knows not why
the lines are there
she knows no roof
apart from the sky
sees no walls, no limits, no boundaries.

# Dreaming

Wasps of sunlight buzz
around late apples.
golden autumn warriors

Apples Hear the sun
light striped pink gold with wasps
buzzing late autumn

Sunlit apples wear wasps
fizzy golden warriors Warriors
drunk on Autumn

Sunlight wearing wasps
buzzes among late apples
Gold, drunk with autumn

Autumn buzzes gold
drunk with late, blushing apples
the echoes of wasps.

*Is this all you've done???*
*You spend too much time dreaming.*
*See me at playtime!!!*

## Seven Wonders

I am small, waiting
for a January dawn
and wondering about

dark and cold glass
and the endless gaze
of the man in the moon

and the stars falling
as thick white flakes
and where the sun

and grey sky might
hide and how it would
feel to be as tall

as my father and
what a strange thing
it is to be born

how just seven years
before – I was still
inside my mother...

# The Shadow

Jenny Drew has eyes of blue
witty, bright and pretty too
writing neat, she's always sweet
snow white socks on dainty feet
top in all the spelling tests
at everything – always best.

Wendy Drew, eyes deep as pools
mud attracted to her shoes
smudges ink across the page
bruise on knees, elbows grazed.
If you blink you might miss her
in the shadow of her sister.

# Shadowland

Here we walk on people,
it is they who follow us
or stretch out ahead like elastic.
How we laugh
        to
         see
          them
            grow
              tall
              pouring
                them-selves
                    down
                        kerbs, shrinking
                            at
                            noon.
                  Here it is they who are grey,
                      we who wear rainbows.

# Miss Rose's Pockets

What have you got in your pockets, Miss Rose?
What is it that's hiding there?
It's flappy and scratchy, fire and cloud
the smell of fresh blisters, brimstone and fear

*Only a mountain covered in trees*
*and under the mountain a cave*
*inside it a dragon with smouldering scales*
*shush, don't make a fuss or he'll wake*

What have you got in your pocket, Miss Rose,
hidden away in the dark?
It's toothsome and hairy, hateful and howl
the stink of full moon, of stalking and stare

*Only the night sky salted with stars*
*and under the night sky, a moor*
*beyond it, a werewolf with ebony fur*
*quiet, not a sound or he'll hear*

What have you got in your pocket, Miss Rose,
where no one else can see?
It's sloppy and slimy, sneering and scowl
the stench of the seashore, dreadful and drear

*Only the ocean murky and deep*
*and across the ocean, grey waves*
*beneath it a monster, all weedy and drown*
*be still or he'll steal you away*

What have you got in your pocket, Miss Rose,
buried where no one can tell?
It's glitter and sparkle, green smoke and spell
with a whiff of newt's eye, whisker and purr

*Only my fingers, knotted and old*
*and light in my hand a wand*
*inside it enchantments, secrets and charms*
*so hush, or I'll turn you to stone*

# Fears of the Unknown

Bad things that might happen tomorrow
Spiders living inside your banana
Monsters that are the same colour as dark
Polar bears hiding in a white towel
Peas that turn into green caterpillars
Drawer burglars who steal single socks

Warm wet shoes when you have a new puppy
Sticky stuff in your anorak pocket
Jumpers knitted by ancient maiden aunts
Door ghosts that inhabit your dressing-gown
Raisins you ate that might have been flies
Things that fall into your mouth whilst sleeping
Suddenly sneezing when drinking hot soup

(writing a poem with only thirteen lines...)

# Chrysalis

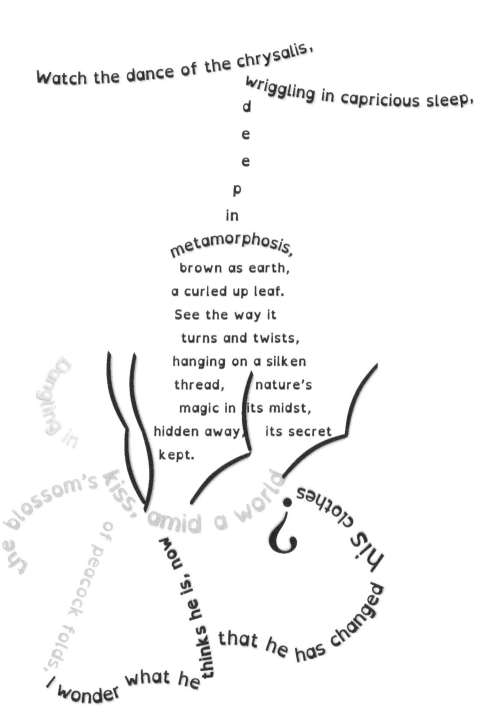

Watch the dance of the chrysalis,
wriggling in capricious sleep,
d
e
e
p
in
metamorphosis,
brown as earth,
a curled up leaf.
See the way it
turns and twists,
hanging on a silken
thread,    nature's
magic in its midst,
hidden away,    its secret
kept.

Dangling in the blossom's kiss, amid a world of peacock folds, his clothes.
I wonder what he thinks he is, now that he has changed

# Taking Care of Small Things

Today I feel tall
so big that I could
jump high above trees
leapfrog a lamppost
step on the sun's toes
catch a plane by the tail
dance up on the roof.
Today I feel tall
yet I love the small
wee, wild things that crawl
snails loving the rain
those worms on their way
I take care with my feet
tiptoe on wet paths.
And besides, who knows
maybe tomorrow
I will feel smaller
grass – impassable
the meanest anthill
seem insurmountable
but just for today
I feel strong, so tall
everything's possible
I wish that I could
somehow bottle it
to drink on small days
and when you felt that way too
I'd give some to you.

# The Camel

The Camel often has the grumps, because he's burdened with two humps, a back that much

resembles lumps, or a nasty case of mumps.
He also runs with graceless thumps and he's
unwieldy when he jumps. Likewise his neck
bent at the front, appears slouched or simply
slumped. Whilst his voice is largely groans and
grunts, with breath that stinks of mouldy pumps.

| His | teeth | | are brown | as |
| old | tree | | stumps, | hair |
| that's | rather | prone | | to |
| clumps. | No | wonder | | he |
| in- | spires | goose- | | bumps, |
| when | he | feels | | he is |
| made | from rubbish | | | dumps... |

# Midnight Owl

I had taken her for mottled ellipse
white moon mist, grey hauntings
of dusk fragments.

The slatted sky she had stitched
fell into silence
under her feathers.

She brushed me with paper wings
rustled like ears of wheat
beneath dark trees

softly rats in their silver shrieked
through parched leaves; her
call looping-eerie

pinched bone notes whisper of night
dredged and coppiced
starlight creeps.

Somewhere in the wood she unpicks life
where her sharp lullaby –
brings endlessly sleep.

# The Swan

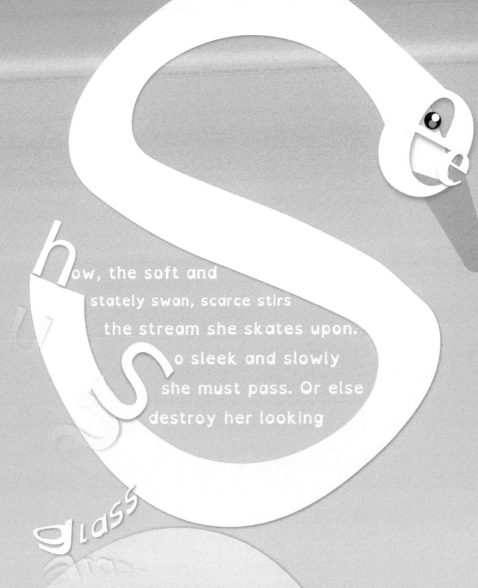

how, the soft and
stately swan, scarce stirs
the stream she skates upon.
So sleek and slowly
she must pass. Or else
destroy her looking

glass

38

# Cork

This leaf in the embers of life
glows hot
on the cold forest floor
remembering the tunnel of mother tree
the soft voice of damp sunlight
how it called to her sweetly.

How the moon watched her begin
far up
above the bark of fox
bathed in the warm scents of a silver spring
the awakening to owl and star
how sky unfolded her neatly.

This leaf etched lichen and rime
her root
laid beside her ear
recalls her whispering sisters, silky, green
the midday humming of bee time
how the gentle wind blew weakly.

How butterfly tickled her chin
and sun
tasted of amber dawn
spreading petal dew and spiced swelling seed
the sap pulsing in fluid veins
how the cork foot grew subtly.

This leaf wrapped in skeletal ice
is mute
as the stiffening earth
gone are her emeralds and yellow paper
weeds
she recalls the falling night
how first she danced, to be free...

## The Colour of Leaves

All summer the leaves
have spoken green words
verdant shadows
dappled sunlight
their voices bitter apples
shade for birds
now they whisper crimson
yellow ochre
some hang on alone
damp and forgotten
others ride the wind
trying to fly south.

## Dog Reads the Wind

He sniffs loose pages, soil characters
earth and leaf are his poetry
Sanskrit dries on mud bark borders.

Swift shifting sky words, grass letters glow
where fox washed her thin feet
on the frosty, autumn meadow

or heron's comma slows a river.
Mole's prologue – his full stop hole
cloud's grey paragraph of feather.

Dog savours mist's enjambment
badger printing on banked clay,
tangs of worm where sparrow fledged.

Beneath the hedge his chapters begin
a smudge of sluggish hedgehog
hare's heels or breeze clips kite's wing.

A mousey caesura. He reads their tails
stories written by the wind; knows well
how to sit behind it – leaving no trace...

*Sanskrit is an ancient language of India used in epic poems.*

# Zephyr

l am the wind and l go where l please
the roar of the storm
or the breath of the breeze
l pay no fare and l travel alone
bending the air and chilling the bone

l am the wind and l roam where l may
the song of the dunes
or the crash of the wave
l ask no leave and l suffer no moods
battering cliffs and buffeting gulls

l am the wind and l go where l must
the howl of the moors
or the keen of the wolf
l give no toil and l ask for no toll
scattering leaves and rattling doors

l am the wind and l go where l like
the voice of the gale
or the cry of the sky
l need no love and l feel no pain
for l rule the clouds, call forth the rain.

# Why Trees Whisper

Why do the trees whisper?
The girl says, the girl says.

It's the sound of their kisses,
the birds say, the birds say.

Not to wake sleepy fishes,
the stream says, the stream says.

So the moon hears our wishes,
the leaves say, the leaves say.

It's a tune the wind whistles,
the sky says, the sky says.

Some say they hate whiskers,
the fox says, the fox says.

I've heard they're suspicious,
the earth says, the earth says.

No it's when they miss us,
the bees say, the bees say.

It's because no one listens,
the trees sigh, the trees sigh.

Oh why do trees whisper?
The girl says, the girl says...

# Monkey Lullaby

Hushaby, monkey child
do not wake in the night
the hunter's asleep now
and the moon is bright.

Do not cry, monkey child
there is nothing to fear
those sounds are the forest
shedding bright tears.

Do not shy, monkey child
the night is your friend
just cricket and fox bat,
not the voices of men.

Do not sigh, monkey child,
now the day is long gone
it's only sky's thunder,
not the sound of a gun.

Ask not why, monkey child
for how should I know
who's heavy of footstep
and cuts their way through.

Rock-a-by, monkey child
in your blanket of leaves
for you need not trouble,
whilst there are still trees...

# The Kenning of Pike

Address him:
Dearest
Pike do not even whisper
Snot Rocket or Slimer, to the
shark of sluggish water. Talk not,
of body-bites or stickle-backed schem-
ing,
for mild mangling of minnows, may yet seem demeaning.
But to a Shaman of shallows don't say Slough Snake or Jack fish.
Sing of shackled smiled loathing for boorish and brackish. Revere
ribald manners with innovative gleaning don't revile the rude delights
of riverbed cleaning. Name him: Lordly Pike for his million years knowing,
he's an uncommon assassin of mardy mouthed maelstrom but don't call him Old
McGraw or Mr Toothy Long Head, ask not why he's quick when all else is slowing. Call
him: King of the lake, praise his weed, water ambush, commend cannibal ways
under tree roots and thick brush, ignore picking off corpses
by bridge pile places, but never speak of
Sharp- tooth or Pointy-nose,
Gater let the brown river
rust on his secrets
for ever...

# If You Could Taste Music

If you could taste music
what flavour would it be?
Might whispers of waves
be salty or sweet?
Would a crash or a bang
be sharp as a lemon?
What if the tang of birdsong
lingered on the tongue?

If you could smell a rainbow
would its odour be faint
might the stars' aroma
fill the sky with scent?
Could the tick of a clock
be the sniff of a sock?
What if some words went off?
Or smelt of wet dog?

If you could touch a dream
how would that feel?
Could wishes be warm
despair cold as steel?
Should shouting be lumpy
and questions be bumpy?
What if ideas felt watery
and lies all crumbly?

And if you could see time
how would that look?
A minute might be pale
some days quite black.
Does hope appear briefly?
What colour is poetry?
What if thoughts could be seen?
Well that might be
er...tricky...

# Fearing Shadows

Yo u
th ink
I'm afr-
aid of
my own
sha dow
since it just
comes and
goes as it
pleases. Trap-
ped, it grows an
angry cat's soul
though it's only
a bit of dark. I'm
fearless see! Let it
hide itself beneath my
feet, not much of a van-
ishing trick at all. Still
I don't like it colluding
with trees, as if it thinks
that it's one of them or
a wall. I may jump
when it sneaks up
behind me, emerging
triumphant after
the rain, when
it enters empty
rooms shiftily
then after I've
gone, pretends
to remain. It
seems it's
most active
in the
evening, now
and then, it waits
upon the stairs. I
feel much safer
once I'm sleeping
and it creeps in
to night and
disapp...

# The Fool's Gold

He asked for treasures from the earth
so I brought him the skull
of a long dead bird
with not a feather on it still
yet once it soared and sang and flew
*what thing is this?*
he says
*a dirty old bone throw it away!*

He asked for treasures from the sea
so I brought him the shell
from an ancient snail
curled up in its pebble cell
yet once it lived and quietly moved
*what thing is this?*
he says
*a dusty old stone, throw it away!*

He asked for treasures from the air
so I brought him the smell
of a summer breeze
dropped from a cloud that fell
yet once it danced and softly blew
*what thing is this?*
he says
*an empty old jar, throw it away!*

He asked for treasures from the dark
so I found a silver bell
and a sparkling ring
yet if they were I could not tell
but I thought it best that he never knew
so I buried them deep
and safe
beneath some old gold, then ran away...

# Dog Explains the Moon

The moon is an apple
said rat
see how it changes from rosy to blue
so fat and ripe
it must taste most sweet
only those who have tasted it truly know.

Oh what rubbish is this?
said toad
you must all see, it's a shimmering pool
so round and full
of glittering fish
it's their diamond scales that change its hue.

I never heard such tosh
said hare
in fact it's the eye of a fearsome wolf
so fleet and wild
with teeth made of stars
its pelt is darkness and its manners cruel.

Oh what nonsense is that?
said bat
to be sure it's a silver moth you fools
so soft and stout
that it sleeps all night
on wings made of light that barely move.

This is but idle talk
said cat
for it is a saucer of cream in truth
as thick and warm
as any might wish
yet once every month again it is full.

Oh no that's not it
said dog
for isn't it strange that it has no smell?
but one day soon
it will surely fall
and then – when it does I'll be waiting.

o !
o
o
o o
o
o o
o o o Who

# Rising Stars

Imagine a child made of long dead stars,
stars that sang ageless and sweet starry songs
shimmering light in galaxies far
so long ago, before a world was born.
Picture skies where they glittered alone
burning to dust their hot starry hearts
see red embers cooling their hoary flame
free falling and spinning through endless dark.
Imagine this child so ancient yet young
what secrets they hold in their starry eyes
a glittering child who walks in the sun
with the ghost of a universe inside.
You may think I lie, though my words are true?
And that child was me and is you and you...

*All life on earth came from carbon which originated*
*from the stars that began the universe.*

# Moonshine

So ancient moon,
what have you seen?  Far
distant and so high.   Whose but
yours, are the words of stars,  set in the
ever changing sky? You heard the first rains
falling, when sea and earth was new, shone down
in the silence on what swam and crawled and flew.
Your smile has ruled the heavens,  of dinosaur and
moth and as the rains turned into snow,  still quietly,
you watched. You knew mammoth and Neanderthal,
lit paths from woods to caves,  beamed on as people
flourished, saw the first small sparks make flames.
You waxed on cities growing, on battles won and
lost. You waned as walls fell over,  returned to
ash and dust. You shimmered   softly over
seas, kept faithfully our nights, alone
among the stars until, one  by
one, came on,  the lights

# Earth Gazing

There once was a girl who lived in the moon
with eyes dark glass, that glittered with stars
but her dreams were colours, a rainbow's hue
and they warmed her soul, her silver heart.
She wished on the sphere of bluest green
for spells to walk in the smile of the sun
and a darkling horse with a midnight mane
on a shimmering path made bright with song.
Then far off she flew, away from the night
to where seas were true and flowers grew
and across the sky on a beam of light
fast, fleet and far, the silver moon maid flew
till her eyes seem blue and her hair as gold
and her soul wore the flames of morning cloud.

There once was a girl who stared right back
with tawny brown eyes and buttercup hair
but her dreams were silver, whispers of ash
full of the moon with its sad lonely air.
She wished on a star dazzling darkly
for spells to walk, far away from the sun
and her soul fell cold, yet burned brightly
as she danced away to where night spun.
Lost from the lands soft with meadows and trees
to where earth is grey and the sky just black
and she twinkles now over moon-pale seas
thin as shadow with the world at her back
with eyes of glass, full of glittering stars
alone with her dreams in the diamond dark.

# Message from a Blue Planet

In the beginning all was black
Red spoke slowly in the darkness
'I will be ripe berries, robin will wear me
where there's dew I'll leave rubies.
Who else but I can raise with the sun?'

This being done the first day hung back
Orange said with a magma voice
'I shall be blaze and honey, fish will wear me
where I go I'll drip amber.
Who but I shall greet the first dawn?'

Yet still the first morning felt some lack
Yellow sighed with buttercup lips
'I'll bring saffron and bee, lion will wear me
where I go will glow topaz.
Who but I can make the daybreak come?'

But day looked sadly at the grass
Green whispered 'Oh how dull it is
I'll give leaf and soft stem, tall trees will wear me
where I go there'll be emeralds.
Who but me should dress field and wood?'

'But what of the water?' Day asked
Blue rippled gently 'Think on this
I'll paint sea and river, sky will wear me
where I have been you'll find sapphires.
Who but I is colder than snow?'

'What of dusk?' the first Day laughed
Indigo sang 'I will bring rest
I'll breath mist and shadow, bat will wear me
yet where I've laid there are diamonds.
Who but I can lift up the moon?'

Then White smiled; rainbows danced
Red, Orange, Yellow grew, Green shoots crept
Blue dropped jewels on wet meadow and tree,
Indigo shadows fell joining mountains
then darkness fell and it was good...

# Out of this World

The Hotel Earth warmly welcomes you
windows boasting a zillion views.
Pets? Well of course and countless creatures
from large blue whales to amoebas.

Just picture urban meets natural
freshly carpeted in every hue.
All accommodating diverse climes
from baking desert to snow and ice.

Try our quiet ocean, languid pools
all with free access to sun and moon.
Subterranean or sky levels
and treetop vistas for daredevils.

Also offered – a wide menu
all diets catered for it's true.
Open all hours, lots of room to park
galaxy rating: six thousand stars!

## In Praise of the Seagull

Let's
hear it f●r the
seagulls, undeniably cool
and if a little
too modest
never needlessly
cruel. Let's hear it for
their talent for litter bin dining;
their stylish table manners and perfect
timing. Let's hear it for their singing, so
shy and retiring, the delicate sound of their tuneful free
styling. Let's hear it for the seagulls, dedicated
and skilful, who delight

in          the

mess      left
by lazy   people

# How Doth the Little Carrier Bag

*After Lewis Carroll. Sadly marine wildlife often mistake
carrier bags for jellyfish and swallow them.*

How doth the little carrier bag
improve the ocean wave
and aren't the tiny fishes glad
of groceries on sale!
How restful is the 'sleeping' gull
stuffed with shiny things
it's good he has a belly full
far more adorns his wings!
How well it makes the turtle grin
wrapped around his jaws
aren't mercury and cadmium
a blessing for us all!

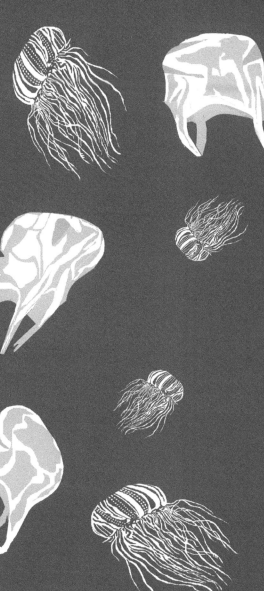

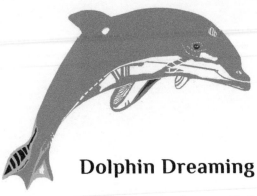

## Dolphin Dreaming

Gliding a seamless path from sea to sky
dolphin dreams green crystals snap in sunlight
he touches air; paradise where he flies
swims here in its mirror of water salt

and when he looks far below him he sees
the small brothers of moon orbiting stars
he knows what's real only sensual deep
knows the thin sea above for a mirage.

Dolphin sleeps in flames of mercurial comets
and when he wakes there are gilt mackerel cloud
murmurations; coral constellations
he has been to the edges of earth-round

and has seen no serpents nor even dragons
only the sail fin fish spinning blindly
have made him doubt he dreamt up people
gliding a seamless path from sky to sea.

# The River Monarch

His dominion is that of otters, velvet voles, plebeian rats. Brown river's flood-fouled-sons in mud colours, hair-shirts. His right is that of ermine collars, to preen his starry, sapphire sleeves or pull threads from his fishing jacket of russet silk, aquamarines. His carpet is that of sunburnt petals water-boatmen, growing fat, scarce pricking at the water's deep-dark-murk. His castle is that horns gather, oars of daub and wattle, moat swollen; drawbridge breached, to hold his court of tiny gallants, wiping minnows from scabbard beaks.

# Crocodile

Just below the moon-chocolate river
as primal as mud, his callused freight
one with the thickened knots of current.
Amber glitters in the labyrinth quiet.

Sinking the sharp stones of burial mouth
bringing white ribbon zebra to water
cloven with plane dust, the thatch-stars of hoof
among the giddy blind roots of mica.

He slips by the clay feet of elephant
earthy tremors of hunched buffalo
to wait his logging in burgeoning silt
half eyes tasting the fettered shallows.

A rock-faced island drifting afloat
flint-lock muscle, primed nostril breath
heaves with sudden jaws of Jurassic plate
and the elegant gift of perfect death.

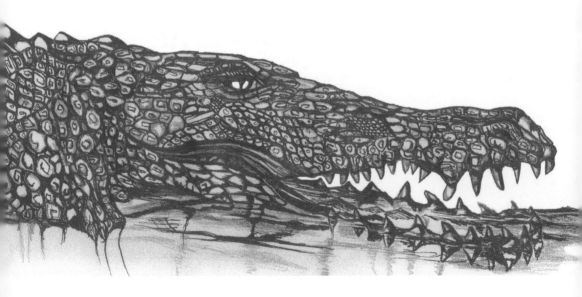

# Peacock

Peacock's

jewels are

sacred

eyes.

One

hundred

stars on

midnight skies.

Robed in morning's

crystal beads,  the

emerald mantle  of

forests, deep  and

where he walks,

exquisite,

rare,

the rustle

of silk on a

marble stair. A

maharaja in disguise

wearing his cloak

of butterflies

# The Writing of Rat

Write him crouched in dark
fire his eye with a spark.
Fill a barn with his scream
mark him miserly mean.

Start scoundrel, add scourge
bring a brigand's foul curse.
Hold loathed to the light
make him noxious with night

Suggest, sour, sneak-thief's sting
allow heinous, hoodwinking.
Allude to gnarled nails
the sly snake of his tale.

Use the bane of his name
imply odour of grave.
With some malice bring fears
plague, pestilence, tears.

Carve out crafty, cruel teeth
hint at simmering grief.
Make a fright of his frown
then scratch out his scowl.

Boil with bold, blaggard's dish
douse with deadly dervish.
Bring a bard and a poem
so he leaves you alone.

*Historically, in Ireland, it was believed that rats
could be warded off by the reciting of poetry.*

# Writing Exercise

First pick up any stray words you find about you.
Just a few at first, say enough to fill a child's tongue
'small' or 'large' is fine, anything polite will do.

Avoid those that are heavy or too long.
Know that it is a far better thing
to use even the tiniest words regularly
than it is to shout disestablishmentarianism once
on a Tuesday afternoon then go to sleep.

To increase stamina remember 'and'
or 'a' are equally as useful as 'happy'
which although appealing may bounce about giggling.
Note: 'gloomy' whilst more grounded may be unhelpful.

'Punctuation' should be dissuaded from shouting.
Discourage compound words like 'light-hearted'
they may take off without warning.

Only use age appropriate language
never take words out of the mouths of
babes and sucklings
or old ladies at bus stops
unless you are any of the above.

Once you have mastered these simple rules
write all your words down quickly before they escape
don't leave the house without paper and a pen
unless there's a fire or you're being chased by dinosaurs.
Never eat your words it makes no nutritional sense at all.

## The Page

This is the page where a poem should be
full of beautiful words and imagery, but
no, turn around, there's nothing to see.

This is the page where a poem wasn't born
its stanzas lie empty, scattered, forlorn. Look
somewhere else, if you can't bear to mourn.

This is the page where no poem could stay
its own metaphor for nothing to say, here
marks the spot, where no marks remain.

This is the page that no poem would touch
it left naught behind, not a crease or a smudge
a complete lack of form, is all we can judge.

This is the page where a poem was once lost
without nouns or verbs, nor even full stops, so
come on then look... Ah well! Perhaps not.

# Found Poem

I found this poem
at the edge of dusk
where a jewelled beetle
kissed green buds
words – in the wind from the spring songs of bird
in a cat's yellow stare
I found this poem

I found this poem
beneath wall and streetlamp
along the long shadows
of riverbank
words – tumbling out from rhythms of dark
in an otter's mud lair
I found this poem

I found this poem
in a fragment of shell
on a footprint of silver
left by a snail
words – written by moth whilst under moon's spell
in a fallen tree's prayer
I found this poem

I found this poem
at the edge of dawn
where light took a brush
to the grey lawn
words – yet unspoken awaiting their turn
in a silence I hear
I found this poem

# Some Poets

Some poets are loud, they jump and they shout
use different voices
caper about
wear bright neon socks
like you to clap

but no, I'm not a poet like that

Some poets are quiet, hate a riot
they may give you 'the look'
seem self-reliant
just hang out with books
commune with cats

but no, I'm not a poet like that

Some poets play songs or bang bongo drums
they can strum a guitar
yodel or hum
they reggae, hip hop
sing blues or rap

but no, I'm not a poet like that

Some poets are bards, they will take to the boards
Shakespearian players
at sonnets – stars
they love a good drama
disguises, hats

Mews!

but no, I'm not a poet like that

Some poets are timid, only a whisper
they conjure up sunshine
snow in winter
charmers of birds
butterflies, bats

but no, I'm not a poet like that

Some poets just dream and stare lots at trees
a little forgetful
fond of the sea
scribbling words
on the bus in the bath
What, am I a poet like that?

Well perhaps...

# If I Were Other Than Myself

If I were liquid
crystal falling up
squeezed by cloud's fist
to fill, where darting fish
and silty weed
soup at heron's feet
then fleet and rich
rise sapphire from the sea.

If I were vast and still
as oceans deep
I'd sing a distant song
of coral reef
rise up to greet
an otherworldly sun
tumbled green
by waves that rage or leap.

If I were as light
as whispered air
I'd ride the tunnels of the wind,
turn stone to drop
where small things creep
upon the moor
on midnight wings
I'd keep the forest's care.

If I were far below the earth,
sensed by touch
the taste and colours
of the soil
pebble-smooth
dwelling secretly beneath
a loamy mirror
to the life above.

If I were infinite
in space and time
could hold a universe
of glittered-stars
afloat about the planet's
swirling paths
dancing from Saturn's rings
to bitter Mars.

If I were other than myself
some part of water, soil or air,
how would it be
to walk or swim or fly
in other spheres
and should I, so wish, would I be missed?

## Forfeit

He said − to prove you love me
go climb the farthest mountain
bring from its peak
a piece of sky
still wrapped, in pale blue cotton.

He said − if you care about me
pluck me a phoenix's feather
prime its quill
with dragon tears
then, write me enchanted letters.

He said − to show real feeling
I, must walk across an ocean
and weave a net
of diamonds, to catch
fish, from a mermaid's fountain.

He said − if you plain adore me
bring the fall, at the world's end
give me the moon
set stars before me.

I said − *let's just be friends.*

# The Songs of Rainbows

*After Henry Wadsworth Longfellow*

When the rainfall softly shimmers
turns my whiteness into rivers
red harvest moon, molten heavens
orange clouds on summer evenings
yellow mist from quiet mountains
leafy green with forest rhythms
icy blue as glacial morning
indigo in shadows falling
dew on early violets fading.

Then I arc across horizons
dance bright on the grey horizon
wearing light made bright with prism
always elsewhere, far and distant.

# Truth and Lies

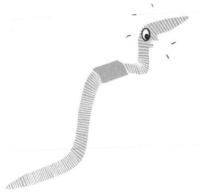

Worm says he loves mud
nice to eat
rain makes it good
but Bird is bad
poking his nose in
lightning wing – swallow him
ask worm how Bird sings
more like rainfall above

Bird says he likes Worm
that he's so sweet
but in turn
that Cat is mean
with his sharp-tooth grin
shadow thin, shapeshift skin
ask Bird how Cat is
more slippery than Worm

Cat says he loves Bird
right to his tweet
but he's heard
that Dog's absurd
all sniffing yapping
bite him, vigour and vim
ask Cat how Dog seem
more stupid than Bird

Dog says he likes Cat
just for a treat
not a chat
prefers them fat
and Bird – everything
but Worm, unappealing
ask what Dog loves best
mud is where it's at

# Promises

They promised rain and winter came
edged with glitter; puddle, stream
stripped the wood of amber shoal
red and yellow wreathes of leaves.
They promised cold and winter closed
nipped fat buds, blackened weeds
swelling flood till rivers rose
covered up restless seeds.
They promised gales and winter came
tore loose branches from the trees
icing meadow, hill and slope
buried clumps of huddled sheep.
They promised snow and winter dozed
sat thick and heavy on the fields
spun with silver flakes to float
falling soft and silently.
They promised hail and winter came
pelted mountains, rolled the sea
filled up lakes, chilled and froze
left the torpid fish to sleep.
The promised thaw and winter roared
swore that it would never leave
held the earth beneath its cloak
sent the sun away to weep.

# Meetings

I met a girl of hazel
her legs were long as sapling oaks
and briars were her fingers
pretty lichens for her nose
she took me gently by the hand
and said some words both green and wise
and all the bluebells of the wood
were in her weeping-willow eyes

I met a girl of water
her voice was soft as waves on stones
and shingles were her fingers
polished pebble for her nose
she took me gently by the hand
and whispered words both grey and wide
and all the fishes in the deep
were in her rocking, salty eyes

I met a girl of winter
her hair was white as sleet and snow
and icy where her fingers
a frozen pond for her nose
she took me gently by the hand
and whistled words both cold and wild
and all the blizzards in the storm
were in her bitter, frosty eyes

I met a girl of fire
her arms were flaming sparks and coals
and magma were her fingers
a glowing comet for her nose
she took me gently by the hand
and crackled words both hot and dry
and all the stars in the sky
were in her burning molten eyes

I met a girl of nothing
her face was naught but dream and moan
and shadows were her fingers
a breath of air for her nose
she could not take me by the hand
here words were lost to all but I
and all the empty things in space
were hidden in her lonely eyes

London...................................................
Leeds.....................................................
Newcastle............................................
Plymouth..............................................
Edinburgh...........................................
Skipton.................................................
Harrogate...........................................
Bradford..............................................

# Trains of Thought

Trains count their days in drumbeats and rhymes
the rhythms of rail are their measure of time

speeds of suitcase races when first they arrive
units of laughter and the numbing of minds

quotas of tree trunks versus telephone lines
the angles of winds and the turns of turbines

numbers of starlings against clouds in the skies
percentages of pylons to billboard designs

distances travelled from a frown to a smile
papers multiplying the figures for crime

the tallies for trollies that sway down the isle
the sum of sheep shivering out on hillsides

a relative value for towns rushing by
records of lost branches, the demise of flies

scores for those sleeping or just closing one eye
cross-sections of tunnels, their shape and their size

the closeness of others approaching behind
gradients of deep valleys and steep inclines

the volume of voices raised in surprise
distortions of Tannoys and musical chimes

the addition of places on bold platform signs
till subtractions of people form fractions of night

in the absence of work trains will ponder and sigh
on the mass of the moon and the scale of starlight

will dream on in rhythms of drumbeat and rhyme
of slowing to stations – and reluctant goodbyes

# Shadows of Doubt

Doors that disturb your dreams
with tall tales of unturned keys
taps dripping away rest
wandering with bold footstep.

Windows strumming black trees
seem to stare mysteriously
words you said without care
echo in the chill night air.

Someone whispers, then leaves
a monster lurking in the eaves
mornings wished away
repeat themselves in shades of grey.

Vents that beg walls to speak
stairs shifting under unseen feet
the doll lost long ago
tells stories of a bin; alone.

Your fears, left in the park
follow you home in the dark
that child you dread to meet
stealing the hours whilst you sleep.

# Pylons

Here edging cities tall and strong
grow rows of pylons on and on
primal circles, standing stones
giants to their metal bones
sullen knights, hardwired skulls
rooted and symmetrical.

Where hedge meets fields and none belong
toughen, tempered, in legion
titan plates of steel and bolt
murmuring with fizzing notes
brooding tapping out a code
inch by inch along the road.

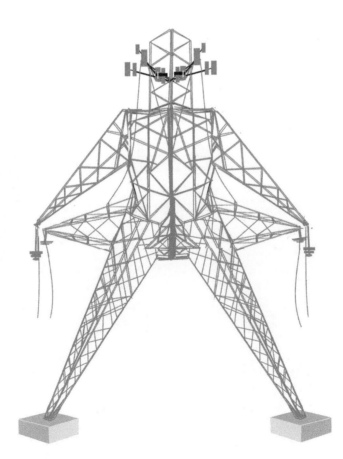

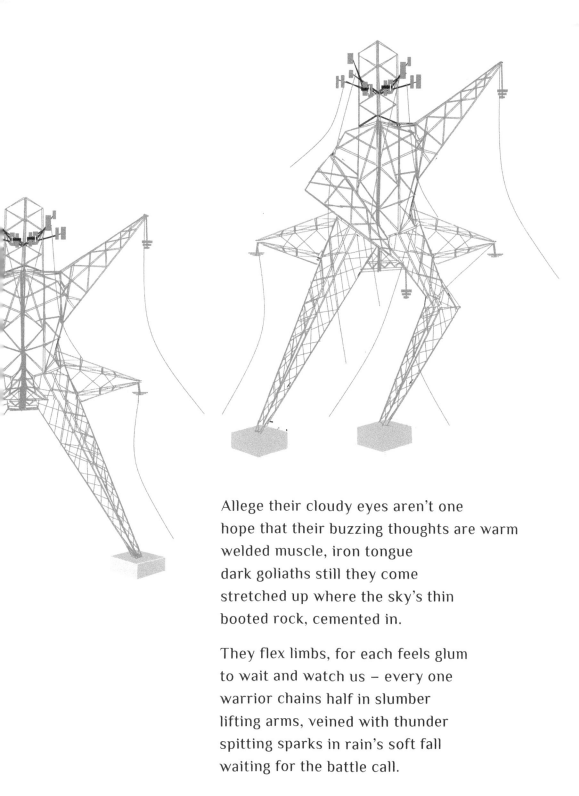

Allege their cloudy eyes aren't one
hope that their buzzing thoughts are warm
welded muscle, iron tongue
dark goliaths still they come
stretched up where the sky's thin
booted rock, cemented in.

They flex limbs, for each feels glum
to wait and watch us – every one
warrior chains half in slumber
lifting arms, veined with thunder
spitting sparks in rain's soft fall
waiting for the battle call.

## Blackout

Now dark creeps in to conquer
filling houses, branches, trees
dwelling in damp alleyways
bleeding into roads and streets
glass becomes obsidian
twinkling rivers ebb with jet
shifting shadows fold, unfold
arches, doorways – spreading nets
one by one the lights come on
lightning commas pausing night
square on square pricks black with gold
cities bloom and skies ignite

## Night Light

Oh who is afraid of the big bad dark?
No – not its colour
blackness is nothing
who fears the coal in the grate
the sleek caress of a raven's feather.

Ah but surely you know it's not sharp
there's no bite to night
the moon has no sting
it is only the vaguest of shapes
being itself in the absence of light.

See how it is pricked by the stars
how it hides indoors
in bottoms of bins
bring the light of a candle – it breaks
look how a window can cut it in squares.

And you must know that it does not stick
no one has come home
with dark on their feet
rooftops and fields aren't covered in stains
night's rain falls like jet – yet is clear by dawn.

No it can't be what lies underneath
they are sacred things
that watch those who sleep
it's only the sound of wind on the planes
no nothing to fear in a moth's wisp wings.

Do not be afraid of the big bad dark
it is most unfair
has no claws, no teeth
it is soft and safe, a tender place
whatever you fear – it does not live there.

# Bedtime Story

She turns the page, climbs inside
away from where day's monsters hide
the minutes tick away unheard
on paper hills of printed words.

She walks the echo of a stair
and sleeps on pillows made of air
dreads no dragons breathing paint
or witches cursing her in ink.

The story lion cannot roar
there is no lock on magic doors
fine leaves of silver, leaves of gold
will never fade or fall to mould.

Each night she goes when she can
wanders through imagined lands
a creature of another's pen
the only words she fears

'THE END'

# SUE HARDY-DAWSON

is a poet & illustrator. Her debut collection,
*Where Zebras Go*, was shortlisted for the 2018
CLiPPA prize. Sue's poems and teaching resources
can be found on the CLPE website. Her second,
*Apes to Zebras* co-written with poetry ambassadors
Roger Stevens and Liz Brownlee, won the North
Somerset Teachers Book Awards. Sue has a First
Class Honours Degree, loves to visit schools and
she has worked with the Prince of Wales Foundation,
Children and the Arts. As a dyslexic poet, she enjoys
encouraging reluctant readers and writers.

*Follow her on Twitter @SueHardyDawson*
*Book a school visit with Authors Abroad*